UNDERSTANDING RADIOACTIVITY

SOME BOOKS BY LORUS J. AND MARGERY MILNE

Nature's Clean-up Crew

The Senses of Animals and Man

Water and Life

The Crab That Crawled out of the Past

Because of a Tree

The Balance of Nature

The Mystery of the Bog Forest

The Biotic World and Man

A Shovelful of Earth

Because of a Flower

Dreams of a Perfect Earth

The How and Why of Growing

Nature's Great Carbon Cycle

Understanding Radioactivity

UNDERSTANDING RADIOACTIVITY

by Lorus J. Milne
and Margery Milne
illustrated by Bruce Hiscock

Atheneum   New York

Special thanks for assistance with the manuscript to
University of New Hampshire associate librarian,
Professor Diane R. Tebbetts. Also to
Professor John Carroll, Professor Edward Chupp,
Mary Chupp, Diana Carroll, Joan Holt,
and other colleagues at the University of New Hampshire.
And to our editor, Marcia Marshall,
who so patiently worked over the manuscript.

Text copyright © 1989 by Lorus J. and Margery Milne
Illustrations copyright © 1989 by Bruce Hiscock

Atheneum
Macmillan Publishing Company
866 Third Avenue, New York, NY 10022
Collier Macmillan Canada, Inc.
First Edition
Printed in the United States of America
10 9 8 7 6 5 4 3 2
Library of Congress Cataloging-in-Publication Data
Milne, Lorus Johnson.
   Understanding radioactivity/by Lorus J. Milne and Margery Milne;
   illustrated by Bruce Hiscock.—1st ed.   p.   cm.
   Bibliography: p. Includes index.
   Summary: Examines the nature, sources, problems, and uses of
radioactivity.
   ISBN 0-689-31362-4
   1. Radioactivity—Juvenile literature. [1. Radioactivity.]
I. Milne, Margery Joan Greene. II. Hiscock, Bruce, ill.
III. Title.
QC795.27.M55   1989
539.7'5—dc19
88-7382 CIP AC

"You can never do a kindness too soon, for you never know how soon it will be too late."

—RALPH WALDO EMERSON

Contents

UNDERSTANDING RADIOACTIVITY

Chapter 1
The Magic
of the Atom

We can't see radioactivity. We can't smell it, taste it, feel it, or hear it. To understand what radioactivity is, we have to begin with the atom. The universe, Earth, and all living things (including people) consist of atoms in various combinations called molecules, which form rocks, oceans, microbes, plants, and animals.

Atoms of nearly a hundred different kinds (elements) have been discovered. At ordinary temperatures and pressures, those of hydrogen, helium, chlorine, and a few others are gases. Those of mercury are pourable as a liquid. Those of carbon, iron, aluminum, and sulfur are solids.

Atoms are smaller than anything we can imagine, about one hundred-millionth of an inch. A measuring device finer than any ruler is needed to measure them. We might think of ten-thousandths of an inch, as a machinist does when he measures a sheet of metal or plastic with a micrometer. That is still huge compared with atoms.

We can use a slicing machine to cut very thin sections through the tissues of a plant or an animal and use an electron microscope to study slices that are only 0.000001 millimeter "thin" (surely not thick!). Anything smaller gets into sizes that ordinary light cannot show us, because the light itself has a dimension—a wavelength—that gets in the way.

The British physicist Sir Ernest Rutherford discovered that the atom has a nucleus with units of positive electrical charge, called protons, and sometimes units without charge, called neutrons. For example, inside each atom of hydrogen is a nucleus with one proton and no neutrons. Each atom of helium has two protons and two neutrons.

Electrons orbit the nucleus somewhat as the planets in our Solar System orbit the Sun. The electrons contribute very little to the weight of the atoms, but they carry half of its electrical charge. The atom has a negatively charged electron for each positively charged proton.

Different forms of the same element may have different numbers of neutrons in the nucleus. They are called isotopes of the element. The various isotopes of the element have equal numbers of protons and electrons but different numbers of neutrons. The total

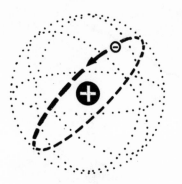
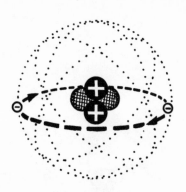

hydrogen atom   helium atom

The nucleus of the hydrogen atom has one proton and no neutrons. The nucleus of the helium atom has two protons and two neutrons.

number of those parts added together gives us the atomic weight. The number that follows the name of the element, for example, uranium 238, shows that the atomic weight is 238. It has ninety-two electrons, ninety-two protons, and fifty-four neutrons. In nature, different forms of uranium occur. One form has an atomic weight of 235, another of 237, depending on the number of neutrons.

You may not know it, but you are "seeing" electrons in a television set. At the back of the picture tube is an "electron gun," which produces a beam of loose electrons. It is focused on the television tube face after being redirected and perhaps filtered to give us a color picture to watch.

Most atoms in nature are stable like the helium atom. Others are unstable because extra neutrons give them extra energy. They are said to be "radioactive."

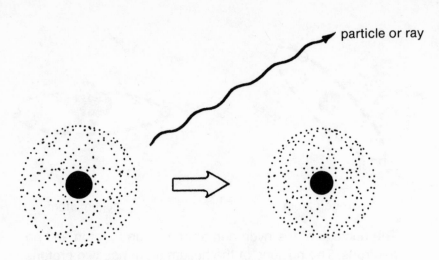

particle or ray

radioactive atom   stable atom

Radioactive atoms lose extra energy by releasing particles or rays until they are stable.

In nature radioactive atoms become stable over time by getting rid of the extra energy. The energy may be carried away from the atom in particles or as waves.

Atoms that are not normally radioactive can be made so by scientists with a machine called a cyclotron, an "atom smasher," or an accelerator. A magnet is used to speed up atomic particles with surges of electricity. At top speed they are aimed and shot at target material. The accelerated particles hit the target atoms with enough energy to smash into their nuclei, changing them to different elements, which can be radioactive. The atoms are smashed much the same way you would shatter a pile of stones by throwing a rock at it.

Chapter 2
Unstable
Atoms

The atoms of stable elements are just as they have always been for more than 5 billion years, since Earth was formed. Different atoms have joined and broken apart many times to make many different molecules, but the elements the atoms form are still the same. Unstable atoms, such as those of uranium and radium, change to a series of other unstable forms, losing energy at each step until they become stable atoms. Uranium atoms release energy at a steady pace to turn step by step into atoms of stable lead. Like a genie from a bottle, the decaying atoms get rid of some energy and take a new form—for a while. Then some more energy comes free, and the atom takes another form, until at last it reaches the final condition, with no more energy to release.

UNDERSTANDING RADIOACTIVITY

No one knew about those changing atoms until near the end of the last century. Then the French physician Antoine-Henri Becquerel made the discovery. Like so many dramatic discoveries in history, this was an accident. Becquerel put a rock of pitchblende in his desk drawer, where he also stored some undeveloped photographic plates. He found, to his great surprise, when he developed the plates, that a large black spot was visible where the ore had been. The obvious conclusion was that the rock contained some unknown element that gave off energy, which behaved like light in blackening his photographic plate. That led to the discovery of uranium in the ore and the penetrating radiation it produced, which earned Dr. Becquerel a Nobel Prize in 1903. Atoms of uranium were the first to be recognized as radioactive.

The energy emitted by uranium spreads out or radiates in all directions. It is called radiant energy, or radiation. It travels at the speed of light (186,000 miles per second) and can pass through such barriers as paper, clothing, and even the human body. Becquerel learned early of the damaging aspects of radiation after carrying a small amount of radium in his pocket. He developed a severe flesh burn near the pocket that held the radium sample. The German physicist Wilhelm Conrad Roentgen studied the rays and called them X rays because their nature was unknown.

This mysterious radiation challenged three of the world's most resourceful scientists: The Polish-French couple Pierre and Marie Curie and their

Pierre, Marie, and Irene Curie

daughter, Irene. Working with pitchblende at the Sorbonne in Paris, they learned to measure the output rays from uranium. They also noted one other element whose radioactivity they could measure in addition to uranium: thorium.

Too late the Curies learned how dangerous radioactive materials are. Pierre died in a traffic accident, but both Marie and Irene became victims of radiation. They developed fatal blood cancer (leukemia), because radiation had affected the blood-forming cells in their bone marrow.

In America Hans Geiger and Hermann Müller devised a special instrument (a "Geiger counter") that detects and registers the level of radiation with audible clicks. The number of clicks per second increases with a rise in radioactive output. With such a device they could detect the amount of radioactivity in any area or object.

Careful measurements with a Geiger counter have shown that radioactivity is everywhere in small amounts in the atmosphere, fresh water, plants, animals, the soil, and the sea. We have always lived with such "background radiation." Probably our ancestors tolerated it for many generations, without noticeable harm. What people today must be wary of is increased levels of radiation, to which the body is vulnerable.

Atoms of uranium occur in varying quantities throughout the crust of Earth. The earliest known source of uranium-containing ores, pitchblende and carnotite, were found in rocks at Joachimsthal in Czechoslovakia. About 93 percent of Canada's known reserves of uranium ores are located in the Blind River area of Ontario. In the United States, deposits are found in New Mexico, Wyoming, Colorado, and Utah. Australia has 27 percent of the world's uranium—in Queensland, South Australia, and the Northern Territory, mostly within an area 136 miles west of Darwin. And together, South Africa and its neighbor Namibia may have another 36 percent of the world's known uranium reserves.

Because decay—the release of energy and particles—has been going on since Earth was formed, only about half of the original uranium in Earth remains. That half will take about 4.5 billion years to diminish again by 50 percent. The time needed for half of a sample of radioactive materials to change into something else is called its half-life, and scientists have used that to measure the length of time an unstable element needs to decay to a stable one.

The decay of uranium 238, which has a half-life

Radioactive Decay of Uranium

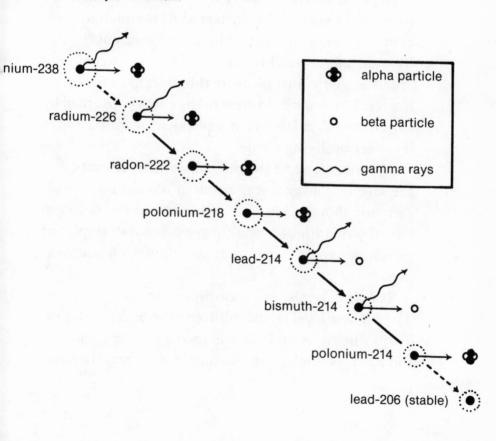

nium-238

radium-226

radon-222

polonium-218

lead-214

bismuth-214

polonium-214

lead-206 (stable)

alpha particle

beta particle

gamma rays

of 4.5 billion years, occurs through a series of steps until it eventually becomes radium 226. It takes another 1,620 years for half of radium to undergo a further change to the gas called radon 222. Radon is much more short-lived, needing only 3.8 days for half of it to become polonium 218. Half of the polonium 218 vanishes every 3 minutes to become radioactive lead 214. Each 27 minutes half of the lead 214 turns into bismuth 214. In 19.7 minutes more, half of it becomes radioactive polonium 214. Then, half of polonium 214 goes on to become stable lead, in less than a second.

As radiation travels away from radioactive material, some of its energy is transferred to the matter it encounters along the way. The transfer of energy can have an effect on this matter. The "roentgen" and "rem" are units that measure the effect of radiation on matter. The roentgen refers to the energy absorbed by matter; the rem (roentgen equivalent man) measures its effect on living tissue.

The roentgen and the rem are quite large units. For the sake of convenience, we often use the milliroentgen (one thousandth of a roentgen) and the millirem (one thousandth of a rem) instead. Some examples of radiation exposure per year are shown on the next page.

Radiation levels vary according to the environment. The highest level (1,500 millirems) of background radiation in rocks and sand is in the Kerala region of India. It is higher in mountainous areas because

Examples of Radiation Exposure
per Year

.1 millirem = expected average dose in the U.S. from nuclear power (1 mile away)

5 millirems = expected average dose for "populations" from nearby nuclear power plants (at the boundary)

40 millirems = average dose from medical diagnosis, such as X rays

100 millirems = average "natural" background radiation, including "natural" uranium, radiation from space, and radiation from all bombs and tests

500 millirems = legal exposure for minors working in nuclear plants and for the general public

5,000 millirems = for special adult nuclear personnel

---

there is less air to block cosmic radiation, and it is intense near the north and south poles.

The most important types of radiation from radioactive substances were given names from the Greek alphabet by Ernest Rutherford. Alpha rays are particles consisting of two protons and two neutrons identical to the nucleus of the helium atom. Starting out at high speed, they lose energy rapidly while traveling through any gas, liquid, or solid and come to rest with zero energy after going through a few centimeters of air. As the radioactive element radium decays, it releases 37 billion alpha rays per second per gram. This amount, called a curie, has become the unit measuring radioactivity and is used to describe the output from other sources as well.

Beta rays are created by a change within a nucleus itself, in which the proton or a neutron breaks down, releasing a positive or negative electrical charge. Composed of high-speed electrons, beta rays are light in weight and move at high speed. They can penetrate paper barriers, but not lead, and can affect a photographic film as though the film had been exposed to light.

Gamma rays have the most energy and can penetrate several centimeters of lead shielding. They are not particles of matter, as are alpha and beta rays, but are a form of electromagnetic energy like light. Thick layers of lead, iron, or concrete are generally required to shield gamma radiation. No normal types of clothing or dress can block it. Some gamma rays are a more energetic form of X rays.

Because radioactive substances emit electrically charged positive alpha, negatively charged beta, or neutral gamma rays, when they penetrate living tissue, they break up (or ionize) atoms in the materials making up living cells.

If this "ionizing" radiation is received at high exposure levels (more than 100,000 millirems in a day, for example), the body can't keep up with repairs very

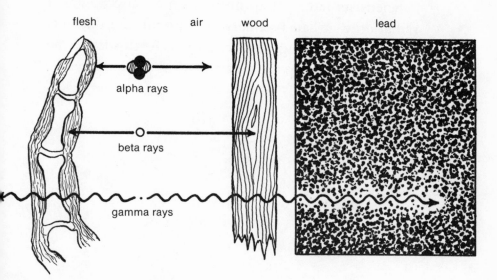

efficiently. A person exposed to such high levels of ionizing radiation would probably show some symptoms of radiation sickness such as nausea and fatigue. But if ionizing radiation is received at low levels, the body does a good job of repairing the damage. A doctor wouldn't be able to detect any medical changes caused by the radiation exposure. Techniques that could detect slight repair to cells have yet to be developed.

But when the radiation exposure at low levels continues for long periods, it might result in the development of an abnormal growth, such as cancer. In the reproductive cells, the egg and the sperm, radiation can alter the genes of inheritance so that the offspring are affected.

13

UNDERSTANDING RADIOACTIVITY

Scientists have yet to find a minimum amount of radiation that can be tolerated without any damage. This includes background radiation. At this time, the actual effect of exposure to radiation can't always be predicted.

Chapter 3
Background
Radiation

Atoms of uranium and other unstable elements produce heat as they change far below ground level. The energy released from them warms the interior of Earth. The energy cannot escape because it is in the midst of solid rock, but it makes the rock warmer. We don't feel the heat at the surface because most of it has been lost in warming interior rocks on the way. From the surface the heat warms the air and eventually escapes to outer space. That leaves the surface of the rock feeling cool to the touch.

In deep mines, though, the air in the tunnel gets so hot that it must be cooled by huge fans if miners are to work underground all day. Engineers must provide 100 to 200 cubic feet of fresh air per minute for each workmen, particularly if the side passageways from the mine shaft are 11,000 feet below the surface. If anything goes wrong and the fans must be turned off, the men have to leave immediately. This air conditioning is needed because of the heat that is released by radioactivity in the rocky walls.

Until this source of heat was discovered, scientists supposed that Earth was still cooling from an original molten condition when the planet came into existence. Now they realize that in billions of years, Earth has had plenty of time to release its original heat. The central core stays tremendously hot—even liquid (molten)—because of the energy released by the radioactive minerals. That core, some 2,000 miles beneath the surface of Earth, is irregular in shape, with liquid mountains and valleys six times deeper than the Grand Canyon. They were discovered in 1986 by means of new techniques assisted by computers.

Because of the heat in the mines, we tend to think of the hot interior of Earth in terms of land areas. Actually, Earth releases heat even at the bottoms of the oceans. Oceanographers who equip themselves to study the sea floor send down sampling devices to measure the "heat flow" from the rocky bottom into the water. The water is surprisingly cold there, because the water of the polar regions has slid down the ocean slopes to the ocean floor. But heat from the interior of Earth is transferred from the sea bottom to the cold seawater. The warm water rises and gets distributed everywhere, heating the seas much more than energy from the Sun could.

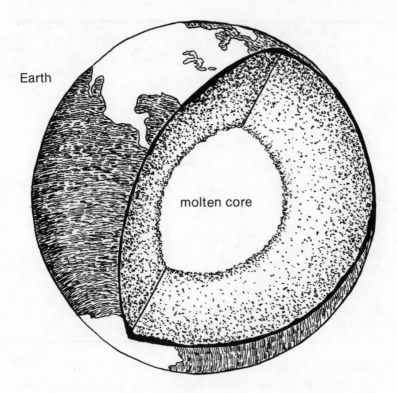

Earth

molten core

Earth has a molten core beginning 2,000 miles beneath the surface.

It is this wonderful supplement of natural heat being conducted outward from within Earth that keeps the surface temperatures within a range that life can tolerate. The warmth from the Sun alone would not be enough for the animals and plants exposed to air and oceans. Our survival on Earth depends on heat from its natural radioactivity.

Everyone is familiar with the radiations that come from something heated enough to become luminous and glow. The glow is light, which is a whole spec-

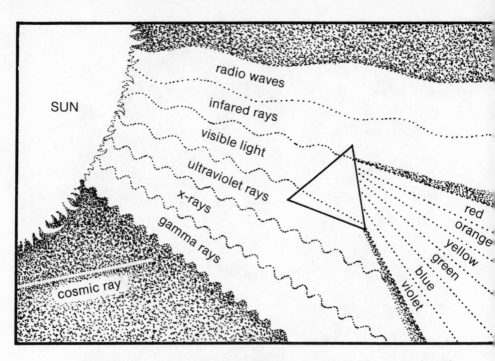

Beyond the range of visible light are longer radio and infared rays and the shorter ultraviolet, X rays, and gamma rays. This whole range of energy is released from the Sun.

trum of energy spread out like a rainbow, a continuous band, from violet through blue, green, yellow, orange, and red, combining to provide us with ordinary "white" light. Beyond that range of visible light, energy waves that are longer are known as infrared, or radiant heat, waves. Shorter ones are known as ultraviolet, X rays, and gamma rays. The shorter the wavelength, the more penetrating is its energy, and the more damage it can do to living things.

The Sun provides the energy of light upon which all living things eventually depend for existence, and it

18

releases this energy at a prodigious rate. The heat at the interior of the Sun reaches 35 million degrees on the Fahrenheit scale. With such heat, the hydrogen atoms in the Sun bounce around at amazing speeds and often come apart.

Every second 674 million tons of hydrogen nuclei in our Sun join or fuse, to become 670 million tons of helium. The difference—4 million tons—transforms into energy, continuing a vast reaction that began about 5 billion years ago.

The gamma rays that are a result of this nuclear fusion produce intense heat, which escapes in all directions, as solar energy. Solar energy is made up of not only light as we see it but also all the other wavelengths of radiant energy. The light from the Sun takes eight minutes to travel to Earth and penetrate its atmosphere. That radiation from the Sun is everywhere and has always been a part of our environment. We are exposed to radiation from outer space as well, from cosmic rays, which are particles of matter produced in the explosions that light the stars.

Cosmic rays may have originated in our own galaxy or in some space beyond our Solar System. The primary cosmic radiation that reaches our outer atmosphere is about 89 percent protons, 9 percent other particles of a cosmic nature from atoms colliding in outer space, and bits of elements from carbon up to and beyond iron. The cosmic radiation that actually meets Earth's surface is changed by the atmosphere and includes gamma rays and electrons.

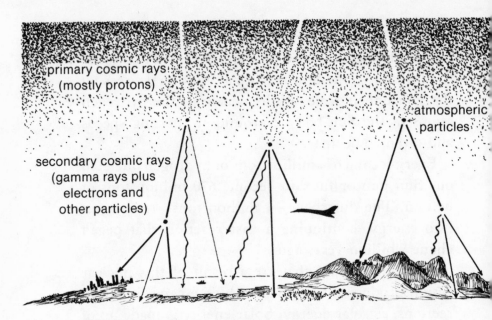

primary cosmic rays
(mostly protons)

atmospheric particles

secondary cosmic rays
(gamma rays plus
electrons and
other particles)

The particles in the atmosphere break up the primary cosmic rays, which are mostly protons, into gamma rays, electrons, and other particles.

Cosmic radiation has been studied and found to have great penetrating power. It can pass through 2,000 feet of water, so its initial energy must be enormous. In outer space cosmic radiation pours invisible piercing particles over everything. Our atmosphere shields us from most of this radiation, but people living at high elevations (Denver, Colorado, for instance) are exposed to more cosmic and solar radiation than are people who live at sea level.

In the same way, people flying in a jet plane seven miles high, or at 37,000 feet, may receive sixty times the cosmic radiation that people on the ground at sea level do in the same amount of time. Cosmic radiation also affects the airline pilot who averages twenty

20

hours a week at 37,000 feet for forty-eight weeks a year and gets greater doses of cosmic radiation than he would at ground-level tasks.

There is no way to escape what scientists call this "background radiation." Small amounts of radiant energy from radiactive materials in Earth itself, plus highly penetrating cosmic rays from outer space, have been bombarding life since the beginning of time.

It is all part of the natural environment. Early cavemen were not aware that the rock walls of their caves might contain minute amounts of unstable uranium, or that they were being bombarded daily by cosmic rays. And in the simple life of earlier times, the radiation levels encountered by man were within limits he could tolerate.

Radon gas is one of the products of the radioactive decay of uranium. We now know that energy particles from radon can affect our lungs. The hazard can build up gradually. Unnoticed, the radioactive radon gas from rocks below a house foundation seeps upward and accumulates in a modern windproof basement. The gas can come from water pouring out of a shower head, if the water has previously become contaminated with radon underground.

In such areas as New England, Florida, and the West, the bedrock naturally contains uranium, which forms radon as one step in its decay. As water is pumped from the bedrock, the radon gas dissipates radioactive particles into the air. When inhaled, they can lodge in the lungs and cause cancer. When radon contamination was found to be widespread in 1986,

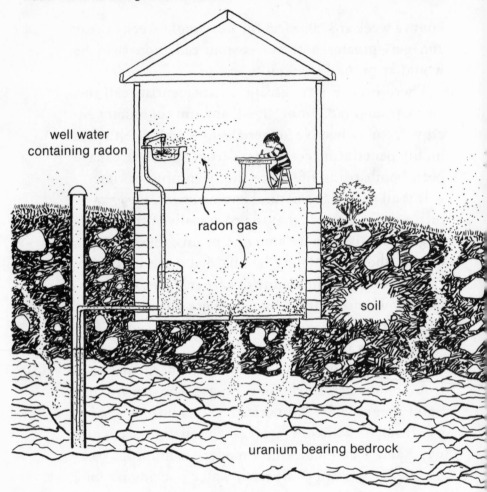

well water
containing radon

radon gas

soil

uranium bearing bedrock

state and local offices assumed the new responsibility of testing for the gas and showing how to get rid of it.

The gas can get into the environment when a house contaminated by radon from soil is ventilated. Sealing cracks in the foundation is one way to prevent radon from entering the house.

At the University of New Hampshire, Dr. Nancy Kinner is conducting research on radon dissolved in water. One way to remove radon involves a system containing activated carbon. Water from bedrock is run through the system, and radon adheres to the carbon. It traps from 75 to 99 percent of the radioactive substances. Solutions result in dilemmas. The buildup on the carbon results in radioactive emissions and also presents the problem of disposing of the radioactive wastes.

Another method of removal is similar to bubbling air through a fish tank. The air bubbles strip the insoluble radon out of the water. It is then vented into the outdoor air. It's a trade-off as to which is the most efficient, cheapest, and safest technique, and the research continues.

The Environmental Protection Agency (EPA) is working on guidelines for acceptable concentrations of radon in air and in water. When the level of radon in the air reaches four picocuries per liter, the EPA recommends lowering the concentration. The average concentration in the atmosphere is three-tenths of a picocurie per liter. A picocurie is one-trillionth of a curie, a common measure of radiation. The radiation from four picocuries of radon could be compared to receiving 200 chest X rays per year and might cause up to fifty lung cancer deaths per 1,000 people exposed. The risk of cancer to a one-pack-a-day cigarette smoker is approximately 150 per 1,000.

The average background radiation in the United

States is between 100 and 200 millirems per year, depending on where one lives and what one's life-style is. Close to half of this is due to radon. Other sources of background radiation besides radon are cosmic rays, naturally occurring radioactive elements in the materials with which we construct our buildings, the air we breathe, the food we eat, and even our own bodies. We also receive an average of 100 millirems a year from medical X rays.

An acute (short-term) exposure of 25 rem (25,000 millirems) would cause little or no immediate biological effect in a person, but it could cause a slight increased risk of contracting cancer in later life.

Dr. Sadao Ichikawa, a geneticist at the University of Kyoto, Japan, has shown that the spiderwort plant, tradescantia, has blue hairs on its stamens. They turn pink when the plant is irradiated, and the proportion of pink hairs is some measure of dosage. The change in color shows up twelve or thirteen days after exposure from a dose too small to be noticed in people for years. The spiderwort test measures the actual intake of radiation, not just exposure, or external, radiation, which a Geiger counter measures. The plant has become a "people's radiation monitor" used in Japan, the United States, and Europe.

Some of the earliest attempts to learn systematically about the harmful effects of radiation were made in a government center called Brookhaven National Laboratories at Upton on Long Island. Dr. George M. Woodwell was in charge. He chose to get his test radia-

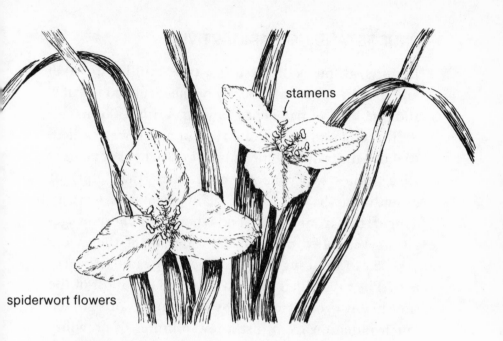

stamens

spiderwort flowers

The stamens of the spiderwort indicate radioactivity by changing color.

tions from a small block of radioactive cobalt. Every night the radiations from it were absorbed harmlessly into Earth at the bottom of a tall aluminum pipe. At dawn, by remote control, the cobalt was hoisted to the top of the pipe and held there until sundown. From the cobalt, radiations spread in all directions, and their effects accumulated day after day.

At intervals the cobalt was kept hidden while scientists on the ground explored to see what remained alive and what had been killed by the exposure to the rays from the cobalt block. Where exposure had amounted to only 2 radiation units per day, all trees and woody plants survived. When the dosage totaled

16 units, all pines died but oak trees still lived. At 40 units, some small blueberry bushes, related shrubs, and one kind of oak kept growing. With 150 units all ordinary plants except one type of sedge were killed. At 1,000 units only some mosses and lichens remained alive. The experiments concluded that upright growth was hazardous for plants. Animals were in danger, too, from lack of food when their chosen vegetation was killed or from the radiation if they were exposed to the rays from the block of radioactive cobalt. The rays killed even ants, which live most of the time below ground level, showing that the ants got too much radiation from just a few minutes of crawling about in the open.

Chapter 4
Energy
from the Atom

Young people today worry about the atom in ways that bothered no one when their parents were eight or nine years old and in the fourth grade. Why is atomic energy so frightening? What makes radioactive wastes so special, so damaging to human lives?

One reason it is so frightening is that the secrets of the energy of the atom first came to the notice of the public when the atomic bomb was dropped in 1945. Scientists discovered that if beams of neutrons traveling about a mile per second are absorbed by uranium 235, they trigger fission (splitting) of the uranium 235 to produce other radioactive atoms and more neutrons. This releases the vast energy holding the particles of the atoms together.

A mere ten pounds of uranium 235, a mass the size

early atomic bomb

At the test of the first atomic bomb in New Mexico, in 1945, a fireball rose up 40,000 feet into the air, surrounded by a giant mushroom-shaped cloud.

of a grapefruit, will produce and absorb so many neutrons and energy that the process continues on its own at dazzling speed and creates an explosion—the force of an atomic bomb. The first test of such a critical mass of uranium was during World War II, on July 16, 1945, atop a tower built in the desert near Alamagordo, New Mexico. While engineers and scientists watched, the reaction started. In a blinding flash the tremendous heat caused the tower to evaporate. The desert sand melted to a thin layer of glass 4,800 feet across, and a fireball rose up into the sky to 40,000 feet, surrounded by a giant cloud shaped like a mushroom. Recording devices gave the scientists a measure of the explosion, as a value they estimated to equal 10,000 pounds of the explosive TNT.

The second atomic explosion was that of a medium-sized bomb dropped from an airplane over the Japanese city of Hiroshima on August 6, 1945. The explosion, equivalent to 20,000 tons of TNT, devastated four square miles of the city, destroying about 67 percent of the buildings, killing 66,000 people, and injuring another 69,000. A third atomic explosion, on August 9, 1945, over the smaller Japanese city of Nagasaki, destroyed a slightly smaller area but killed 39,000 people, injured another 23,000, and convinced Japan to end the war the next day.

These bombs are called fission bombs because they result from the splitting of the nucleus of uranium 235 or plutonium 239. A fusion bomb, on the other hand, releases energy when the nucleus of two atoms combine. Fusion, which is the reaction taking place in the depths of the Sun, requires heat to millions of degrees.

The heat energy produced when radioactive atoms change from one form to the next can be put to peaceful use as well. Within a special building called a nuclear reactor, the heat of the nuclear reaction turns water into steam. The steam can drive a turbine, a kind of high-speed paddle wheel, to generate electricity and provide a factory or a city with light and power.

The heart of the nuclear power plant is the "core," where the nuclear fuel is placed. The energy released by controlled fission does two things: It sends neutrons flying off, some of which strike other uranium atoms and cause them to split instantly; and it produces heat, which can be used to produce power.

Each nuclear reactor is loaded with fuel rods containing pellets of uranium 235 about the size of a lead-pencil eraser. Slender tubes of the metal zirconium enclose the pellets without interfering with the escape of neutrons.

Unless the heat from the radioactive material at the core of a reactor is controlled by cooling devices, it can build up to melt the fuel rods and everything near them—a runaway reaction called a meltdown. Or steam pressure can increase until the insulation of the reactor building gives way in a disastrous explosion, tossing bits of radioactive materials into the air.

On April 26, 1986, a steam pressure explosion occurred at the nuclear power plant in Chernobyl, a town near Kiev in the Ukraine. The explosion was followed by a partial meltdown.

Since an accident at any reactor can release radioactive dust (called fallout), which winds will carry for long distances, the most effective safety precaution is to be miles away from any nuclear power plant. Europeans have not forgotten that the government of the USSR did not report the explosion at Chernobyl until

Nuclear Power Plant

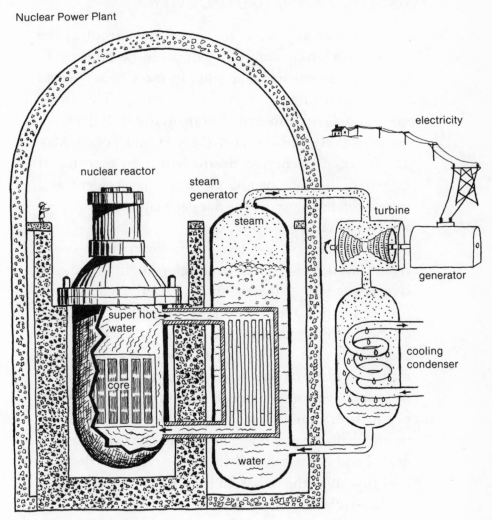

electricity

nuclear reactor

steam generator

steam

turbine

generator

super hot water

core

cooling condenser

water

concrete shielding

after Norwegian scientists, who were thousands of miles distant, routinely monitoring radioactivity in the atmosphere of Scandinavia, announced that a major increase was detected somewhere upwind.

The closer anyone is to a reactor in trouble, the sooner dangerous radioactive dust can be expected to arrive. Fallout from Chernobyl in the USSR reached Switzerland in four days, and it was picked up by sampling devices aboard aircraft flying to India from Moscow (May 2), New York (May 5), and Tokyo (May 11). By then twenty-six deaths had been reported at Chernobyl—those people close to the accident and some who had entered the danger zone to rescue people still alive.

During the first two days, the radioactive emissions from Chernobyl resulted in a high content of radioactive substances in the air and radioactive contamination of the ground. In late 1987 air activity had more or less disappeared, but it occasionally increased when radioactive dust was stirred up from the ground. The radioactive substances from Chernobyl consisted of isotopes of various elements, most of which are fission products of uranium 235. The short-lived substances (with a half-life of a few weeks or less) mostly disintegrated and contributed little to the radiation dose. In mid-June 1987 the radiation level was 15 to 20 percent of the original.

The radioactive substances on the ground mostly gave out gamma radiation. This type of ground radiation was mainly from cesium 135, with a half-life of two years, and cesium 137, with a half-life of thirty years. The cesium will slowly sink into the ground and remain at a depth of a few centimeters. The topsoil will then screen off the radiation.

Cleaning up the Chernobyl nuclear disaster

On April 29, 1986, the USSR chose to relocate all the people who survived the immediate nuclear disaster at Chernobyl. The remains of the reactor itself are isolated under fifteen feet of concrete. Much of it was poured from hovering helicopters that could swiftly get away. Workmen on the ground, trying to clean up the debris, could stay at the site only a few hours each week before absorbing into their bodies more than the tolerable weekly limit of radiation.

Almost eighteen months after the nuclear power station explosion in the Soviet Ukraine, levels of radiation in more than 200 human volunteers in Scotland had not fallen. This suggests that radioactive cesium was still present in food at that time. Vegetarians showed lower levels of radiation than did meat eaters.

In June 1988, thousands of sheep in Scotland and Wales were still affected by Chernobyl fallout. Certain soils in upland areas had retained higher levels of radioactive cesium, in spite of winter rains. The cesium had been stored in roots of grasses and made its way to the leaves eaten by lambs and their mothers.

Researchers stress that levels of radioactivity recorded are only marginally above normal and do not indicate a health hazard. Yet research continues, and contaminated areas are being monitored.

The worry about the dangers of nuclear reactor accidents has to be weighed against the power needs of modern industrial countries. In Europe today France has forty-four nuclear reactors and is building seventeen more; the United Kingdom has thirty-eight, and four more under construction; West Germany has twenty, and five more on the way; Spain has eight, and three to come; Italy has three, and two more being built; Sweden has twelve, Belgium eight, Switzerland five, Finland five, and the Netherlands two.

Of the 145 reactors now producing electricity in Western Europe, 53 are within thirty miles of another country's territory. The Danes, who produce no nuclear power, are well aware that the Swedish reactor at Barseback is just ten miles from Copenhagen, the Danish capital. The Irish, who prefer to make at least half their electricity by burning peat, complain to the British that nuclear danger frightens them from just across the Irish Sea.

In the United States a near disaster occurred in 1979 at the Three Mile Island nuclear power plant some miles south of Philadelphia, when a cooling pump failed and temperatures in a nuclear reactor rose to hazardous levels. One of the buildings was damaged and partly filled with radioactive liquid. Workmen in protective suits are still trying to clean up the building and dispose of the radioactive liquid it contains. An unexpected difficulty was detected in 1986: Bacteria and minute plants are growing in the water, making it so murky that the workmen cannot see what they are doing. The microbes are far more tolerant of radioactivity than are human bodies. Filters intended to clear the water get clogged in twenty minutes and then must be disposed of with great care, since they contain radioactive microbes.

Nuclear power plants also create another problem. In providing the heat necessary to generate electricity, each nuclear reactor annually yields about 8,000 curies of radioactive waste. Only the least dangerous can be released into the environment. The remainder must be stored in some safe way for 500 to 1,000 years—

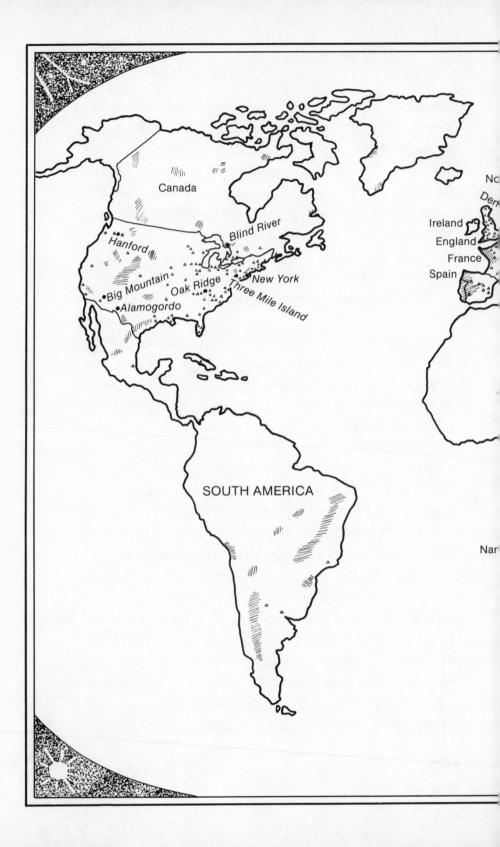

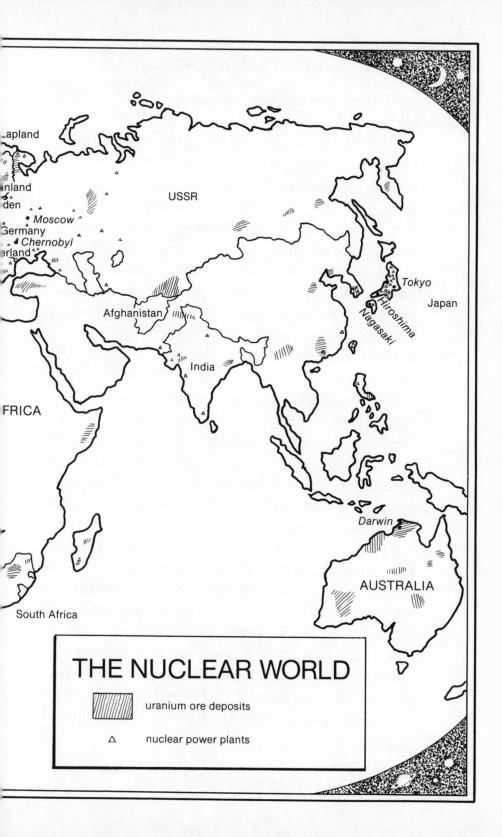

Lapland

Finland
Sweden

Moscow

Germany

Chernobyl

Switzerland

USSR

Tokyo

Japan

Hiroshima

Nagasaki

Afghanistan

India

AFRICA

Darwin

AUSTRALIA

South Africa

THE NUCLEAR WORLD

uranium ore deposits

△   nuclear power plants

until the radiation has decreased to levels that are tolerable.

Various sites have been suggested for dumping high-level wastes. One suggestion is to lower sealed canisters to the sea floor a few hundred miles away from land, where only the deepest nets set by fishermen might catch anything that had been exposed to radioactive leakage from the containers. Another proposed solution is to dump wastes in the still deeper places in the oceans called trenches. But there is no guarantee that anything placed there will go down into the molten core of Earth rather than pass into water currents or into living things that may be eaten by fish that fishermen later catch.

Abandoned chambers of old salt mines may offer storage sites, but then we have the problem that leakage from radioactive canisters might enter groundwater supplies and reappear in drinking water near the surface. "Out of sight and out of mind" does not necessarily mean out of the cycles of materials upon which life depends.

The federal government plans to store high-level nuclear wastes in sites in Nevada, Texas, and Washington State. Because no safe method of storage has yet been found, these sites will immediately be off limits for anyone walking about, driving through, or otherwise exposing themselves to the radiations that might possibly escape from the waste canisters. It is planned that each canister will be sealed within a steel case with a glassy covering, to reduce the likelihood

Drums containing nuclear wastes

Nuclear wastes can be stored in abandoned salt mines.

that the radiation might leak out into the environment.

Radioactive wastes are either high level or low level. High level includes the fuel rods. Low level includes all of the usual trash, disposable clothing, gloves, and clean-up material that becomes contaminated during the running of the reactor.

Seventy-five percent of the U.S. nuclear waste is now stored on a 570-square-mile site at a Hanford facility on the Washington side of the Columbia River. A "criticality accident" occurred in a similar trench full of radioactive waste in the Soviet Union in 1975. Apparently, loss of water in the trench allowed the plutonium there to collect into a critical mass and start a local atomic explosion, showering everything nearby with deadly radiation.

Not only are high- and low-level wastes produced at atomic reactors everywhere, but while each reactor is working for its thirty or forty years, contamination progressively affects its whole structure. Finally it is necessary to shut down and safety-coat the plant, much as was done at Chernobyl in 1986. Each generation of humankind must continue to hope that a less expensive and safer method will be found to retire old reactors, if only to conserve space and manpower.

There is a uranium-rich area fifty miles east of Grand Canyon National Park at Big Mountain. It is a place of endless sagebrush and soaring golden eagles. It is also home to Native Americans. Here the Navajo seem to be in conflict with their near neighbors, the Hopi.

One solution suggested was that the Navajo be moved to keep peace among the tribes. But the idea of relocation has met with resistance. The Navajo believe that the relocation plan is a conspiracy between government and energy companies eager to mine the land, which contain rich seams of coal and uranium. Legend warns them to leave the land alone.

Uranium development seems inevitable, but the ultimate decision belongs to the Native Americans. Uranium development is a one-time use of land. After use, groundwater will be depleted, and air and surface water will be polluted with radioactivity. The land surface will be scarred and pockmarked with tail-ings—piles that require safeguarding for thousands of years. The Native Americans must decide if this de-struction to their lands is worth the price.

Chapter 5
Problems with
Plants and Animals

During World War II American scientists set up a national laboratory in the remote mountains of Tennessee at Oak Ridge. There they devised and produced the highly radioactive materials needed to create an atomic bomb. Work with those materials also resulted in wastes with varying amounts of radioactivity. Some seemed harmless; gases and some tainted gas-borne particles could be released into the atmosphere. Liquid and solid wastes with a greater concentration of radioactivity had to be stored for months or years until their radiation decreased to a level that could be ignored. Even so, there had to be a place to store them.

The scientists planned to dump some of the material from the Oak Ridge Laboratory into White Oak Creek, which empties into the Clinch River. Therefore, to dilute the wastes greatly before they reached any populated area, a dam was built across the creek. It created a pond of about fifty-five acres, not more than eleven feet deep, where wastes would be kept for about a month before they trickled into the creek itself. No one expected any radioactive contamination to escape.

The earliest warning that living things might carry radioactive materials away from the storage ponds came in the 1960s. Turtles, whose bodies had become mildly radioactive from eating contaminated wild foods, emerged from the ponds, the females to lay their eggs, the males to find females. Some males that had been scientifically marked at the storage pond had become radioactive and were found five miles away. It was the same with females, which traveled less but contained more contamination because they lived longer. How far would the material be carried? How much would be concentrated by the turtles' feeding on contaminated plants and then again in the animals feeding on the turtles?

Who would think to blame the minute green plants living in the pond water? Each individual plant is too small to be seen except through a microscope. Who would imagine these plants would live long enough to absorb many radioactive atoms, then be eaten by tiny animals, which would further concentrate the radioactive materials? They themselves became more radioactive than the material they ate. But this did occur, and the tiny animals were in turn eaten by small

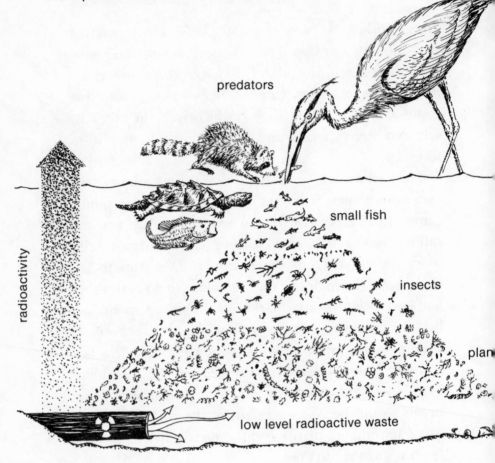

predators

radioactivity

small fish

insects

plan[t]

low level radioactive waste

fishes. Larger fishes then ate the small ones and their radioactive contaminants.

Among the experimental radioactive wastes stored in the pond were compounds containing cesium 137. Cesium 137 decays to 50 percent of its concentration in thirty years, to 25 percent in sixty years, to 12.5 percent in ninety years. It releases both beta and

44

gamma rays at each step in the process. During that time even tiny amounts of cesium 137 have a good chance of being absorbed by minute plant cells, which seem unable to tell the cesium from the potassium 39 they need for growth. Animals of increasing size and life-span take in the cesium 137 with their plant food and concentrate it in their tissues. By the end of the summer, the big bass in the pond had eaten so many of the small fishes that bass flesh held 1,000 times more cesium than did the pond water. At the same time, the concentration of radioactive strontium 90 in the bones of the bass reached a concentration more than 2,000 times that in the pond. The average concentration of radioactive zinc 65 increased 8,720 times beyond that in the environment. This natural process is known as "biological amplification" or "bioamplification." It happens because of the ability of living things to get from their environment all of the scarce substances that are important to them and concentrate them over time within their bodies.

Small fish near the pond surface attract herons, waterfowl, and other fish-eating birds. They gobble up the fishes, concentrating the fishes' radioactive materials in their own bodies. The herons and waterfowl then fly away and spread the radioactivity all over their migration routes. In addition, bird droppings containing radioactive substances contaminate remote water edges, where no one is expecting any danger.

Problems arise also with ground squirrels, burrowing owls, pocket mice, insects, and plants, such as rabbit brush and tumbleweed. With roots that can grow twenty feet, tumbleweeds reach down into waste dumps and take up strontium 90 into their stems and branches. Then they break off and blow around the dry land. Most come to rest in patches of sagebrush. If a fire broke out, the smoke could carry airborne radioactive contamination. The Department of Energy has expressed concern that the tumbleweed could travel all the way to a river and spread the contamination farther.

A badger broke through the security lines at the world's first plutonium factory in 1959. It dug a hole in one of the waste pits. After it left, rabbits began to stop by for an occasional lick of the radioactive salt. Before long, they had scattered 200 curies of radioactive droppings over the 2,500 acres of the Hanford Reserve in Richland, Washington.

This mishap ranks near the top of wildlife disasters because it created "one of our largest contaminated areas," one that remains hot today with cesium 137 (with a half-life of thirty years) and strontium 90 (with a half-life of twenty-five years).

The radioactive materials thrown into the atmosphere from the explosion at Chernobyl have been measured with great care. The amount of cesium 137 from Chernobyl is particularly feared because wind carries the radioactive debris over populated regions and lands where food for people is grown.

Some radioactive substances were deposited on the growing vegetation. Particles became attached to

tumbleweed

Tumbleweeds carry radioactivity and spread it onto other locations, perhaps even to rivers.

sprouting grass, while the remainder, through rainfall, sank into the ground. The radioactive substances on cultivated soil will get plowed down into topsoil. Different things affect the amount of radioactive substances taken up by plant root systems. High calcium content causes a low uptake of strontium 90, but soil with a high content of organic substances (humus) causes an increased amount of cesium to be taken up by way of the plant root systems.

Cows grazing on the contaminated grass will take radioactive substances in their milk and bodies. Cow meat can become contaminated for eating. If people eat the meat and the plants containing radioactive material, it will be stored in their bodies for varying amounts of time. Radioactive cesium accumulates in

47

muscle tissue. The body gets rid of half the accumulation in fifty to seventy days. Strontium accumulates in bone and teeth. It can remain there a long time and have a destructive effect on the bone-marrow cells.

lichens

Reindeer and caribou may feed on radioactive lichen.

A vast amount of the dangerous debris from Chernobyl has been blown northwest by winds and settled on Lapland, a region extending over northern Norway and Sweden. Lowly lichen plants growing in the Far North have absorbed the dust and become radioactive.

Lichens themselves are extremely slow-growing plants, needing years to attain a height of a quarter inch. They are famous traps for radioactive particles, including those brought to the Arctic by winds from the South Pacific, where the early tests of atom bombs were made.

Reindeer (which are Eurasian caribou) eat the lichens and become contaminated, too. Those reindeer, which furnish the principal meat supply of Lapland people, are now too radioactive to be eaten, and the Lapp people are in great danger since the reindeer herds provide their food and livelihood. Sympathetic people in Alaska have been gathering and shipping uncontaminated ripe berries and other food to the Lapp people as gifts.

Many scientists worry about gray marsh birds known as coots, which spend the winter feeding in wetlands in northeastern Africa and the Ukraine. When spring arrives, the coots migrate north through Afghanistan as far as Scandinavia and the arctic tundra in the USSR. Every coot that stops to feed on favorite foods in the Ukraine has a good chance of being contaminated with cesium 137 and other radioactive substances produced and dispersed from the explosion of the nuclear power plant at Chernobyl. Farther along the migration route, Afghans enjoy the flesh of coots as food and could be next in line to take in dangerous amounts of cesium 137. This one explosion released into the atmosphere at least a tenth of the radiation emitted by all the atomic explosions and weapons previously used or tested.

coots

Coots are at the top of the food chain, concentrating radio-activity.

The International Ornithology Congress has called for research on the effects of the Chernobyl accident on migratory birds. The first inquiries should be made by those countries whose bird population uses the Ukraine flyway. Even goose droppings in Holland have tripped Geiger counters. Earlier Albert Schweitzer, the humanitarian and Nobel Prize winner, speaking about the Columbia River near the Hanford installation, warned, "The radioactivity of the river water was insignificant. But the radioactivity of the river plankton (microscopic green plants) was 2,000 times higher, that of the ducks eating the plankton 40,000 times higher, that of the fish 150,000 times higher . . . the egg yolks of the water birds 1 million times higher. . . ." Schweitzer said, "The end of further experiments with atom bombs would be like the early sun rays of hope which suffering humanity is longing for."

While radioactivity from man-made weapons and nuclear power plants is very dangerous, we must realize that Earth was created with radioactive elements. The cockroach has adapted and survived massive doses of radiation for millennia. With a better understanding there is a chance that someday the harmful effects of radiation might be greatly reduced for all living things.

Chapter 6
Other Uses
of Radiation

After the monstrous explosions of atomic bombs that destroyed so much of the Japanese cities of Hiroshima and Nagasaki in 1945, the laboratories that produced the radioactive materials for those weapons were able to make artificially produced radioactive atoms available for nonmilitary purposes. Scientific and commercial uses for those atoms were quickly discovered.

When you are on your way to board an airliner for a national or international flight, you are directed through an arch where weak X rays are used to check that you are not carrying hidden metal that might be explosive. Your luggage goes through a different arch, with stronger X rays, while a technician watches for silhouettes of suspicious metal items to show up on a special fluorescent screen. After you have passed your tests and your luggage is ready, you can sometimes see the fluorescent screen the technician is watching as the luggage of later passengers goes through.

You may be cautious enough to have your films and cameras taken around the X-ray device for hand inspection, because you fear that the X rays will fog the unexposed films or ruin pictures already taken. Audio- and videocassettes should go around, too, so that the X rays will not damage recordings or unused tapes.

The effects of X rays accumulate, which means that if films or tapes are taken through an X-ray machine several times on a single trip, the films or tapes can lose much of what you wanted on them. The effect of X rays also builds up in a person who is X-rayed too often, and this can cause damage.

You may be more familiar with the X rays from a well-shielded instrument in your dentist's or doctor's office. The penetrating abilities of these rays lets them pass through a human body and create a shadowy picture of the inner details, which can be made visible on a fluorescent screen or recorded on a photographic film. The dentist or the surgeon can then see bones and inner organs before or after surgery, just as airport technicians can use their similar equipment to detect metal objects in pieces of luggage without opening them.

When you go to the dentist and the dental technician gets ready to take an X-ray picture of your teeth, you are covered by a heavy apronlike shield, which absorbs any stray X rays that might affect other parts of your body. The photograph is made with the least possible amount of X-radiation, and the technician usually has a shielded place in which to stand while the brief exposure is being made.

Radioactive substances have other beneficial uses in medicine and industry, too. For example, radioactive iodine (iodine 131) can be prepared to be included in a medicine designed to treat problems of the thyroid gland. Radioactive iodine taken by the patient in food or drink finds its way to the thyroid gland and there gives off radiant energy that can destroy such abnormal cells as a cancerous growth.

Minute amounts of phosphorus 32 can be given to plants and animals kept for a while in an aquarium to which this radioactive material has been added. Following the exposure, it is possible to recognize the same individual plants and animals among a wild population that has not been so exposed. They are "tagged" for scientific observation until something eats them and the radioactive atoms are transferred to a different creature.

In the physiology laboratory scientists are able to follow the chemical pathways of ingested compounds that contain radioactive atoms to learn the complex chemical changes that go on in a living plant or animal.

A newer procedure is a tag of radioactive man-made cells that can be injected into the bloodstream of a person who has just suffered a heart attack. Within six to twenty-four hours after the attack, the marked cells

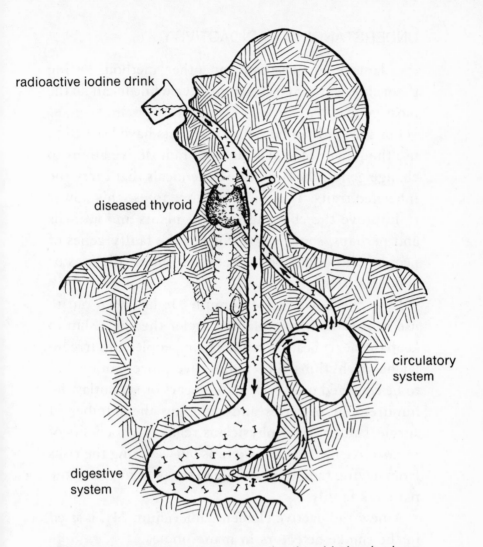

radioactive iodine drink

diseased thyroid

circulatory system

digestive system

Radioactive iodine finds its way to the thyroid gland, where the radiant energy can destroy abnormal cell growth.

attach themselves to damaged muscle in the heart and can then be located by means of X rays. That gives the doctors information about the extent and location of

55

the damage earlier than any other method, letting them choose what treatment to give while it can do the most good.

For the study of heredity, scientists have learned to use the power of radiation from radioactive atoms to change genes, the tiny coded chemicals that carry the inherited traits. The scientists hope to use this power to improve the characteristics of plants and animals and perhaps, someday, to correct the faulty genes of people who might be expected to inherit diseases or abnormalities.

Even the power of plutonium 238 has been put to use in pacemakers implanted under the chest skin to keep the heart beating regularly in people with irregular heart rhythms. The radioactive power source has to be renewed only once in ten years or so, outlasting hundreds of batteries and reducing the number of surgical steps. Most physicians regard the benefits of radioactive heart pacemakers as outweighing the risks from having radiation so close to the patient and to the patient's family.

A new radioactive element, americium 241, is used in the smoke detectors in many homes.

The nuclear submarine, such as the USS *Nautilus*, was first launched in 1954. A nuclear reactor provides the power, enabling it to stay underwater for months at a time. Ordinary submarines have to come to surface to charge their batteries.

Radioactivity can be used to date ancient living things, too. Radioactive carbon (carbon 14) is formed every day in the upper atmosphere, where cosmic rays from outer space strike atoms of nitrogen gas (nitrogen 14) and change the atoms to radioactive carbon 14. In the atmosphere the radiocarbon joins with oxygen gas to form radioactive carbon dioxide, which gets mixed in the atmosphere with nonradioactive carbon dioxide until there is about one of those radioactive carbon-dioxide molecules per trillion of nonradioactive molecules. In their normal process of gaining carbon for growth, green plants absorb both types of carbon-dioxide molecules in this same proportion and maintain this ratio among their carbon atoms so long as they are alive.

After a plant dies, its radioactive carbon begins to decay. Half will have transformed (and half will be left) at the end of 5,770 years, and only a quarter of the radioactive atoms will remain at the end of 11,540 years. This makes it possible to determine the age of a piece of dead plant or animal material by carbon dating—measuring its ratio of radioactive to nonradioactive carbon.

Wood that has been cut to make beams for the roof in ancient Native American houses can be given dates in that way. Carbon in bones of great auks that they caught and ate at a feast along the New Hampshire coast revealed that the event took place in 1739 B.C., nearly thirty-six centuries before the last bird of this kind was exterminated.

Ways are still sought to improve the use of the germ-killing features of radioactivity from gamma rays to

Radioactive Carbon Dating of Wood

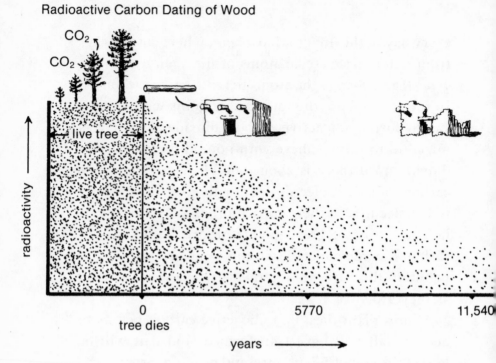

Radioactive carbon, taken in by a tree, begins to decay when the tree dies, so that an object made from that tree can be dated according to the amount of radioactive carbon remaining in it.

prevent food from spoiling. The danger is that the long-term effects are still unknown.

At Fisheating Creek in central Florida, all of the wastes from visitors and campers at a wayside park were made harmless by piping them past a container of cobalt 60 in the center of an enormous concrete cube. Bacterial cells, virus particles, and molecules of organic waste simply broke into harmless fragments when the rays struck them, without any radioactivity being generated in the residue. For years this equipment served the campground, releasing water of extraordinary purity for disposal into the creek. Now an increase in visitors to the park has added more wastes than the system can handle, and other, more expensive devices have been installed.

The nuclear industry is one of the most tightly regulated industries in the world. Yet with all the beneficial uses humankind has found for radioactivity, it still continues to pollute the environment.

Unfortunately we can suffer from nuclear radiation without being aware of the exposure. To avoid destruction of ourselves and our environment, long-term use of radiation requires more research before it can truly benefit humankind. In our reverence for life we need to be fully aware of the radiation cycle, to be able to control it more completely, so that we won't contaminate the natural balance of the biosphere.

Epilogue

Chernobyl Area to Be Ecological Reserve

The Soviet government has decided to designate the area in a 10-kilometer radius from the Chernobyl nuclear power plant as an ecological reserve that will be used to carry out scientific studies of the impact of radiation on the natural environment.

Following the accident at the nuclear power plant just over two years ago, Soviet scientists argue that this information, which will be gathered by a number of special laboratories in the reserve and will involve, for example, tracking the behavior of animals and the growth of plants, could eventually be useful in helping to increase the yield of crops and their resistance to disease.

"It would not be possible to reproduce the ecological situation which has been created in the Chernobyl area by experiment," Boris Prister, chairman of the radiology coordinating council of the southern branch of the Lenin Academy of the Agricultural Sciences, told the Soviet news agency TASS last month.

"Regardless of the tragic nature of the event, scientists have gained a unique laboratory which makes it possible to study the effects of radiation on living nature," Prister said, although adding that "so far no real influence on the genetic apparatus of organisms has been observed."

13 MAY 1988
Science
D. Dickson, vol. 240, p. 877
copyright 1988 AAAS

Glossary

Accelerator—A machine used to study the nucleuses of atoms, by increasing speed of electrically charged particles, breaking them apart to learn their composition. One kind of accelerator is a cyclotron.

Alpha rays—Charged particles made up of two protons and two neutrons emitted from the nucleus of a radioactive atom. Alpha rays are the least penetrating and often travel with beta and gamma rays to give nuclear radiation.

Atom—The smallest unit of an element, consisting of a central nucleus surrounded by orbiting electrons.

Beta rays—Streams of high-energy electrons emitted from radioactive atoms.

Carbon—A chemical that is part of all living things. One of its isotopes, carbon 14, is radioactive and can be used to measure the age of ancient objects.

Cobalt—A silvery metal that becomes radioactive when placed in a nuclear reactor.

Cosmic rays—Particles originating in the stars and interacting with atoms in the atmosphere to produce electrons, gamma rays, and other radiation.

Curie—The unit used to measure radiation. One curie equals about the amount of radiation given off by one gram of radium, or 37 billion nucleuses, disintegrating every second.

Decay—Decrease in radioactivity over time, caused by emission of charged particles or rays from the nucleus of an atom.

Electron—One of three basic building blocks of matter. An electron has a negative electric charge exactly equal and opposite to the positive charge on a proton.

UNDERSTANDING RADIOACTIVITY

Element—A substance that cannot be broken down by chemical action. All atoms of the same element have the same number of electrons. The ninety-two elements in nature, alone or in combination with other elements, make up everything in the world. Hydrogen and carbon are two natural elements. Scientists create artificial ones.

Fission—The process by which an atomic nucleus splits and produces heat energy and radioactive particles.

Gamma rays—Invisible rays of high-energy radiation. The strongest rays given off by fission, they are stronger than X rays.

Geiger counter—An instrument used to measure and detect radioactivity.

Genes—Protein molecules within sex cells that transmit characteristics from parent to offspring.

Graphite—A form of carbon used to accelerate the nuclear reaction in some power plants.

Half-life—The time it takes half the atoms of a radioactive substance to decay to another form. Half-lives range from less than a second to millions of years. After two half-lives, one-quarter of the radioactivity remains.

Ion—An atom or molecule carrying a positive or negative electric charge, as a result of losing or gaining electrons.

Isotopes—Forms of a chemical element with varying numbers of neutrons but the same number of protons. Unstable isotopes emit radioactivity.

Meltdown—An accident at a nuclear power plant in which nuclear fuel becomes so hot that it melts.

Neutrons—Uncharged particles in the nucleus of all atoms except hydrogen. They keep the fission reaction going in nuclear reactors.

Radioactivity—Energy in the form of particles or rays emitted by unstable atoms as they decay. Radioactive emissions include alpha and beta particles, neutrons, gamma rays, and X rays.

Rem, millirem—A measure of the effect of radiation on humans, incorporating dose and type of radiation. One millirem is one-thousandth of a rem.

X rays—A form of highly penetrating radiation. Unlike gamma rays, X rays do not come from the nucleuses of atoms but from their surrounding electrons. Some are barely stronger than sunlight, while others are of great penetrating power.

Books on Radiation

Asimov, Isaac. *How Did We Find Out about Nuclear Power?* New York: Walker & Co., 1976.

Fuller, John G. *The Day We Bombed Utah.* New York: New American Library, 1984.

Grossman, Karl. *Cover Up: What You Are Not Supposed to Know about Nuclear Power.* Sagaponack, N.Y.: Permanent Press, 1962.

Gyorgy, Anna, and Friends. *No Nukes: Everyone's Guide to Nuclear Power.* Boston: South End Press, 1979.

Lillie, David W. *Our Radiant World.* New York: Tab Books, Inc., Liberty House Imprint, 1987.

Pringle, Laurence. *Radiation: Waves and Particles/Benefits and Risks.* Hillside, N.J.: Enslow Publishers, 1983.

Index

Index

Index

plutonium, 29, 39–40, 56
polonium, 9, 10
potassium, 39
primary cosmic rays, 20
Prister, Boris, 60
protons, 2, 20

R
radiation:
  background, 8, 11, 12,
    15–17, 19–21, 23–24
  definition of, 6
  environmental levels of,
    10–11
  harmful effects of, 14,
    24, 25–26
  heat produced by, 15
  ionizing, 12–13
  speed of, 6
radiation sickness, 13
radioactive decay, 9–10
radioactive waste, 23,
  42–51
  animals and, 43–46
  dispersion of, 43, 46,
    49
  explosion caused by,
    39–40
  in food chain, 43–45,
    51
  high level, 39, 40
  lifetime of, 35–38
  low level, 39, 40
  storage of, 35, 38–40

radioactivity:
  animals and, 25–26,
    43–51
  biological amplification
    of, 45
  cells affected by, 12, 13
  dating by, 56–58
  definition of, 3
  discovery of, 6
  food preservation and,
    57–58
  medical uses of, 53–56
  nonmilitary uses of,
    29–30, 52–59
  plants and, 24, 25–26,
    43, 45–46, 49
  release of, as energy, 4,
    5
  tagging by, 54
  waste purification by,
    58–59
radium, 5
  decay of, 9, 10, 12
radon, 21, 24
  acceptable levels of, 23
  contamination by,
    21–22
  decay of, 9, 10
  lung cancer caused by,
    21
  methods for removal of,
    23
reindeer, 48, 49
rem (roentgen equivalent
  man), 10
Richland, Washington, 46

Index

uranium development,
environmental effects
of, 40–41

V

vegetarians, 34

W

Wales, 34
Washington State, 38
waste, radioactive, *see*
radioactive waste
waste purification, 58–59
wavelength, 2
West Germany, 34
white light, 18

White Oak Creek, 42
Woodwell, George M., 24
World War II, 28–29, 42

X

X rays, 6, 12, 18
discovery of, 6
effects of, 53
medical, 24, 53, 55
radiation levels of, 11,
24
uses of, 52–53, 55

Z

zinc, radioactive, 45
zirconium, 30